Cowboys and Cowgirls
Yippee-Yay!

Gail Gibbons

L B

LITTLE, BROWN AND COMPANY
New York   Boston

For Larry, Joan, and Ben Whiting

Little, Brown and Company

Hachette Book Group
237 Park Avenue, New York, NY 10017
Visit our website at www.lb-kids.com

Little, Brown and Company is a division of Hachette Book Group, Inc.
The Little, Brown name and logo are trademarks of Hachette Book Group, Inc.

First Paperback Edition: July 2003

Library of Congress Cataloging-in-Publication Data

Gibbons, Gail.
   Cowboys and Cowgirls: yippee-yay! / [by] Gail Gibbons. — 1st ed.
     p.   cm.
   Summary: Explains and illustrates the equipment, work, and lifestyle of cowboys and cowgirls in
the Old West.
   HC ISBN 978-0-316-30944-8
   PB ISBN 978-0-316-16859-5
   1. Cowboys — West (U.S.) — Juvenile.   2. Cowgirls — West (U.S.) — Juvenile literature.
3. West (U.S.) — Social life and customs — Juvenile literature.   4. Frontier and pioneer life — West (U.S.) —
Juvenile literature.   [1. Cowboys.   2. Cowgirls.   3. West (U.S.) — Social life and customs.
4. Frontier and pioneer life — West (U.S.)]   I. Title
F596.G53   1998
978 — dc21   97-6113

PB 10 9 8 7 6 5

SC

Manufactured in China

COWGIRL

COWBOY

From the 1860s to the 1890s, the Old West was a rough and wild frontier. It was the era of the American cowboy. Not many women lived in the Old West, and there were only a few cow-girls. Besides, at that time, the work of a cowboy was considered too harsh for most women.

Wealthy ranchers owned large tracts of land on which they grazed longhorn cattle. These ranchers hired cowboys, whose lives centered around tending the cattle, rounding them up, and moving them on long cattle drives for sale and profit.

A **WIDE-BRIMMED HAT** protected the cowboy from the sun and rain.

A **BANDANNA** could be pulled over the mouth to keep dust away.

A **VEST** with pockets

GLOVES

Leather **CHAPS** protected legs from cattle horns, rope burns, scratches, and scrapes.

High leather **BOOTS** kept out pebbles and dirt. Pointed toes made it easy to slip the boots into the stirrups.

Some cowboys wore **SPURS**.

A cowboy's clothing was chosen for rough wear and tear. Many cowboys wore the same clothes for months at a time. Some even slept in them! Smelly and caked in dirt, these clothes were often burned after a long cattle drive.

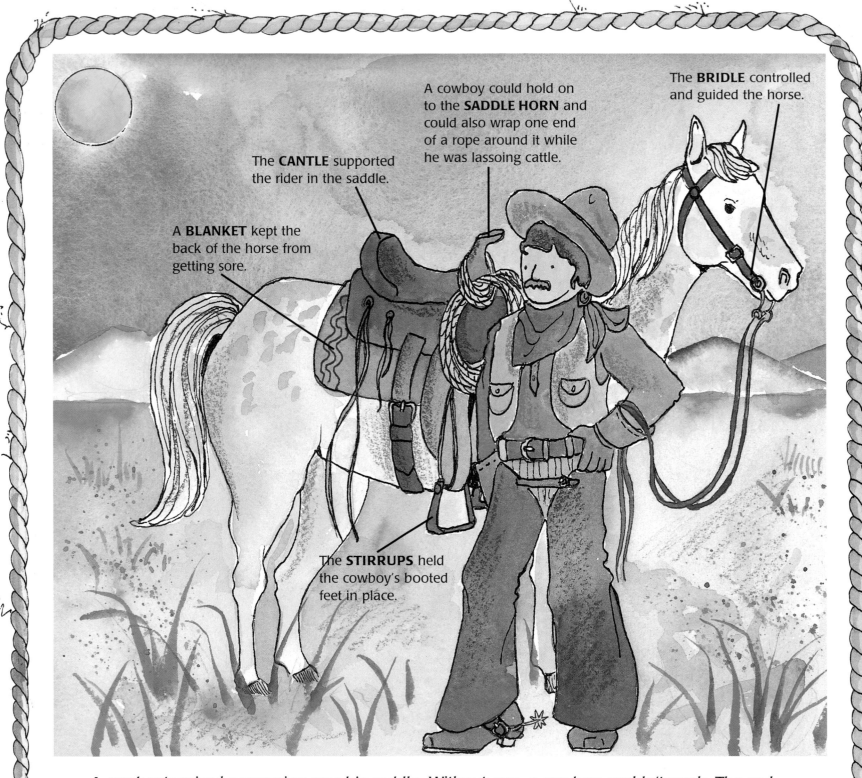

A cowboy could hold on to the **SADDLE HORN** and could also wrap one end of a rope around it while he was lassoing cattle.

The **BRIDLE** controlled and guided the horse.

The **CANTLE** supported the rider in the saddle.

A **BLANKET** kept the back of the horse from getting sore.

The **STIRRUPS** held the cowboy's booted feet in place.

A cowboy's prized possession was his saddle. Without one, a cowboy couldn't work. The saddle had to be comfortable. Cowboys spent much of their time riding horses and ponies owned by the ranchers. Often the horse or pony became a cowboy's best partner.

LARIAT

A short whip, called a **QUIRT**, was used to guide cattle.

A **KNIFE** was important for cutting rope and other material.

Some cowboys had a **RIFLE** or other **GUN** for protection.

A heavy **BULLWHIP** was used to drive cattle out of thick brush.

The **HOLSTER** held the gun.

The **CANTEEN** held water.

Roping was the most difficult skill for a cowboy to learn, and it was the most important. Cowboys carried ropes called lariats to lasso cattle. It took many months of practice to learn to spin the lariat and release it at just the right moment.

A **BRONCO** is a partially tamed horse or pony that bucks.

BRONCOBUSTER

A **CORRAL** is a fenced-in area.

BUCKAROOS were assistants.

Wild horses had to be captured and tamed before they could work among the cattle. A skilled cowboy called a broncobuster would mount and ride the wild horse until it would trot obediently around the corral. What a wild ride! Busting, or breaking, horses was a very dangerous job.

Ranchers were unable to fence in the entire boundary of their many acres of land. So long-horns from different ranches would graze together freely. Once or twice a year, ranches held roundups. All the cattle and newborn calves would be rounded up, or brought to one location.

It was hard work to round up all those critters. Cattle are wild and fast. Any longhorn trying to get away would be lassoed and captured. The cowboy had a loop at the end of his lariat. When he twirled it and let it fly, the rope would snag the animal from afar. No cowboy wanted to get too close to an angry longhorn!

Each ranch brand was registered in a **BRAND BOOK**.

BRAND

When the cattle were finally rounded up, the trail boss from each camp would count his herd.
He could tell which longhorns belonged to his ranch by a mark on his cattle, called a brand.
The calves didn't have brands. They were easy to identify because they followed their mothers.

Some common brands were

The Lazy J

The Flying V

The Scissors

The Quarter Circle T

Next, the cowboys lassoed the calves. This was called chopping out. One by one, the calves were brought to a wood fire filled with heated branding irons. The cowboys took turns pressing a branding iron to each calf's hip, leaving a mark.

Any stray steer within their own herd was lassoed, identified by its brand, and returned to the correct ranch. This was called cutting out.

RUSTLERS

RUNNING
IRON

Cowboys who stole cattle from other ranches were called rustlers. These outlaws used a running iron to change the captured animals' brands to match their own. Pictures of rustlers' faces often appeared on wanted posters, and big rewards were promised for their arrest.

After the roundup came the trail drive. The best and the biggest longhorns would be moved in one huge herd along a trail to the closest town with a railroad station, called a railhead. The cattle were then brought to market by train.

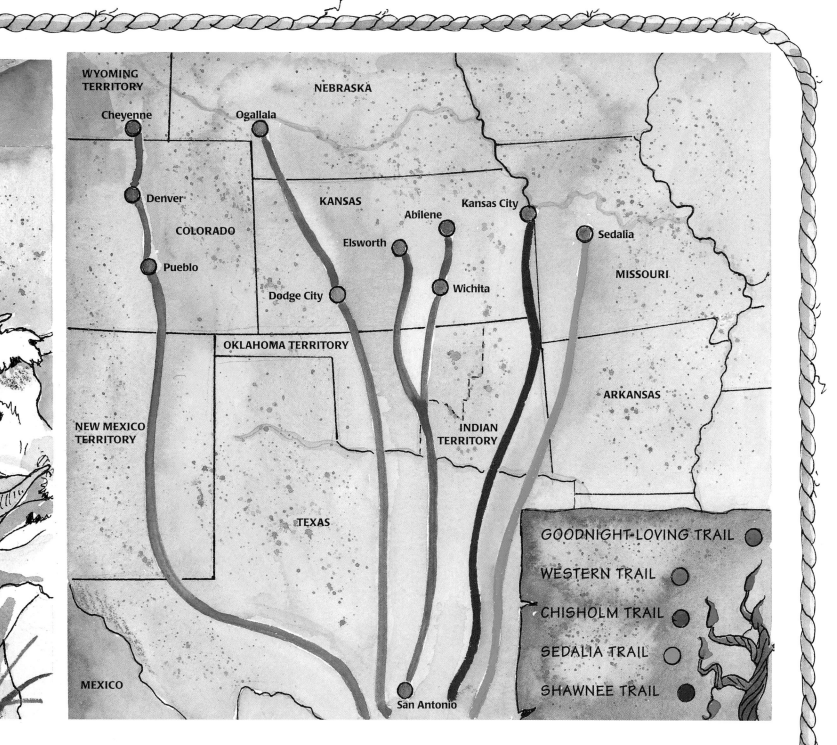

WYOMING TERRITORY

NEBRASKA

Cheyenne

Ogallala

Denver

KANSAS

COLORADO

Abilene

Kansas City

Sedalia

Pueblo

Elsworth

MISSOURI

Dodge City

Wichita

OKLAHOMA TERRITORY

NEW MEXICO TERRITORY

ARKANSAS

INDIAN TERRITORY

TEXAS

GOODNIGHT-LOVING TRAIL

WESTERN TRAIL

CHISHOLM TRAIL

SEDALIA TRAIL

MEXICO

SHAWNEE TRAIL

San Antonio

Some trails were very long, nearly a thousand miles. Cowboys could drive the herd for only about ten to fifteen miles a day. They didn't want to push the cattle too hard, or they would lose weight, and they also took time to stop and let the animals graze along the way. Cattle drives could take many months. Only the toughest cowboys went on them.

COOKIE

CHUCK WAGON

A herd of several thousand cattle might stretch a mile along the trail and be tended by as many as fifteen cowboys. Each cowboy had his own task. The chuck wagon rolled along ahead of the herd, carrying food, cooking utensils, and bedding. Cowboys called food chuck. The chuck wagon was driven by the cook, called cookie.

Next came the wrangler. He was in charge of the spare horses, often numbering as many as one hundred. This group of horses was called a remuda, a Spanish word. The trail cowboys would switch to fresh horses three or four times a day.

SWING RIDER

The trail boss, also called the foreman, rode at the head of the herd. This cowboy had good knowledge of the trail, was able to communicate with the Native Americans they might encounter, and was an excellent tracker. As the cattle in the front of the herd began to move along, the other cattle followed.

TRAIL BOSS
Also called the **FOREMAN**

POINT RIDER

The front of the herd was called the point position. The most experienced cowboys rode as point riders. They guided the steer in an arrowhead shape, keeping the pace and moving them along in the right direction. Cowboys called swing riders moved the herd forward and made sure the cattle didn't spread out too far.

The flank riders kept the cattle within the herd, preventing strays. The rear of the herd was called the drag position. The drag cowboys had the worst job of all. They rode through thick clouds of dust, urging slowpokes along and keeping an eye out for rustlers.

CHUCK BOX

WATER BARREL

Some days the cowboys were in the saddle for sixteen hours—a long, hard day. Because the cookie traveled ahead with the chuck wagon, he was able to have food cooked and ready when the trail team arrived. A meal was usually pork and beans, sourdough bread, and coffee. "Come and get it!" he would call.

The cowboys often joked with the cookie while they ate their meal.

Oh, give me a home where the buffalo roam,
Where the deer and the antelope play,
Where seldom is heard a discouraging word,
And the skies are not cloudy all day.

Home, home on the range,
Where the deer and the antelope play,
Where seldom is heard a discouraging word,
And the skies are not cloudy all day.

Many nights, cowboys would sit around the campfire, telling stories and singing old cowboy songs. It was a time to relax and gaze up at the never-ending sky filled with twinkling stars. Some cowhands used their saddles as pillows when they settled down in their bedrolls to sleep.

Day after day, the cattle moved along the dusty trail. What the cowboys feared most was a stampede. Cattle were easily spooked. Thunder and lightning or any strange noise could send the herd charging in a panic. It was the cowboys' job to get the herd back under control. Many cowboys were injured or killed carrying out this task.

After a long, hard journey, the cowboys and cattle at last made their way into town. The cowboys moved the cattle into pens near the railroad tracks. From there, the cattle would travel by train to points east. The rancher was paid for the steer, and the cowboys were paid for their work. It was time to have fun!

The first thing a cowboy wanted to do was soak in a hot tub. What a treat to get a haircut and a shave and to buy new clothes! The cowboys would then sing, dance, and have fun on the town. The sheriff always stayed nearby to be sure that law and order prevailed.

Back then, cowboys and cowgirls showed off their skills at rodeos—and they still do today. The word *rodeo* comes from the Spanish word *rodear,* meaning to encircle or round up. People in the stands cheer as cowboys and cowgirls compete for prizes.

Rodeos feature five main events: bronco riding, bull riding, bareback riding, steer wrestling, and calf roping. It's a colorful and rowdy scene!

Today, cowboys and cowgirls still tend cattle and have roundups. But the days of the long cattle drives are over. Railroads can now be found near almost every cattle ranch. Many cowhands have college degrees in agriculture and livestock breeding.

Cowhands drive pickup trucks and tractors and sometimes fly airplanes or helicopters to spot stray cattle. Cowboys and cowgirls today are still skilled in roping, branding, and riding horseback, just like the cowboys and cowgirls of the Old West.

Famous Cowboys and Cowgirls

William F. Cody, also called "Buffalo Bill,"

was a famous hunter, scout, and Wild West adventurer. He became known as Buffalo Bill when he formed Buffalo Bill's Wild West show.

Annie Oakley

was a star of the Wild West show and could outshoot almost any cowboy in the West. Audiences applauded the skill and bravery of this hard-shooting, hard-riding woman.

Wyatt Earp

was a famous frontier lawman and gunfighter. He served as deputy sheriff and United States marshal in several Kansas and Arizona cow towns. He is most famous for a gunfight at O.K. Corral in Tombstone, Arizona, 1881.

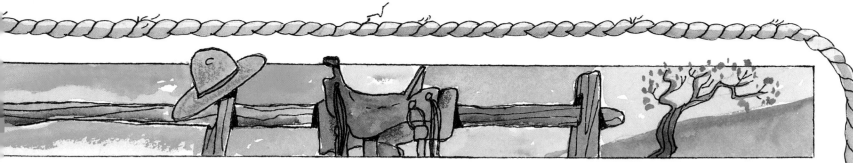

...ll Pickett

...s famous for his riding, roping,
...d bronco-busting skills. He
...came the first African-American
...be enshrined in the National
...deo Hall of Fame.

Calamity Jane

was a famous cowgirl who
claimed to have been an army
scout and Pony Express rider. The
Pony Express was a famous relay
mail service that operated from
early 1860 to late 1861. At one
point, she rode alongside Wild Bill
Hickok. She roamed the Wild
West dressed as a man.

"Wild Bill" Hickok

was a scout and frontier law
officer. He was famous for his
marksmanship and bravery.
From 1872 to 1873, he demon-
strated his cowboy skills in
Buffalo Bill's Wild West show.

Yippee-Yay!

The best-known cowboy hat is the Stetson, called the John B. after its maker, John B. Stetson.

The Texas Rangers were formed in 1835 to deal with outlaws, cattle rustlers, and conflicts with Native Americans.

Between the 1860s and the 1890s, there were about forty thousand working cowboys and cowgirls.

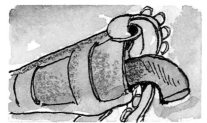

Not all cowboys owned guns. Those who did used them mainly for protection against wild animals.

Cowboys in South America are called gauchos. In Chile, they are called *huasos*, and in England, drovers.

It's not true that cowboys and Indians always fought. Cowboys had more in common with most Native Americans than they did with city people.

The trail boss sometimes paid a toll to Native Americans when crossing their land. They paid as much as ten cents per steer or gave a few longhorns in trade.

The Pony Express used cowboys to run mail between Missouri and California, over two thousand miles of wild country. It ended after eighteen months because of the invention of the telegraph.

The American cowboy has always been a symbol of freedom and bravery.